AF431882

Mystical Zenith:

The Supra-Conscious Mind

Volume 4

Tevin C. R. Dubé

ISBN: 978-976-96823-5-1

Publishers Note

Tevin Curtis Ryan Dubé

Trinidad and Tobago

Email: tevindube@yahoo.com

Facebook Page –Tevin 'Mystical' Dube

Instagram – mystical_dube

Twitter – @mysticaldube

Cover Design by Tevin C. R. Dubé

CONTENTS

Foreword...7

Section One:...11

Section Two:...29

Section Three:...47

Section Four:..65

Section Five:..83

Section Six:...101

Section Seven..121

Foreword

Mystical Zenith: The Supra-Conscious **Mind** contains a further count of a little over three hundred and twenty extremely powerful meditations.

Our main purpose is to discover exactly who or what we are. Our purpose is to wake up unto the fullness of our individual self and see our unique connection to that of the Universe itself.

Never allow the mirages of the finite nature of the flesh to totally distract you from the immortality you are already in possession of. Evolve your thoughts and learn to become One with the infinite All in All.

Divine Love, Peace, Blessings, and Enlightenment of Mind always!

Section One

The beauty behind the madness of our universal creation is Silence. The Absolute Divine is the very Source of meditation in meditation, meditating our entire projection through an internal experience. —Tevin C. R. Dubé

If you want to come to know yourself you must be willing to go beyond your physical identity to discover who or what you truly are from deep within. —Tevin C. R. Dubé

The real journey to the centre of the Earth is actually the voyage and venture to go within your own soul that will help you uncover and unearth the many hidden mysteries within the void of the Spirit.
–Tevin C. R. Dubé

Our Universe is the result of a Divine Sleep and when the Great Awakening reaches its zenith of actualisation, the reality of this existence will no longer seize to be. –Tevin C. R. Dubé

Our existence is nothing more than a beautiful nightmare happening in a sweet dream. –Tevin C. R. Dubé

Only when the cat's away the mice does come out to play. Only when God sleeps, demons and devils roam the street. But when God awakes, imagination gets to take a break. –Tevin C. R. Dubé

It is quite okay to fail but never fail to keep working on becoming a better version of yourself. –Tevin C. R. Dubé

To be alive is a gift but to be able to live is a blessing. –Tevin C. R. Dubé

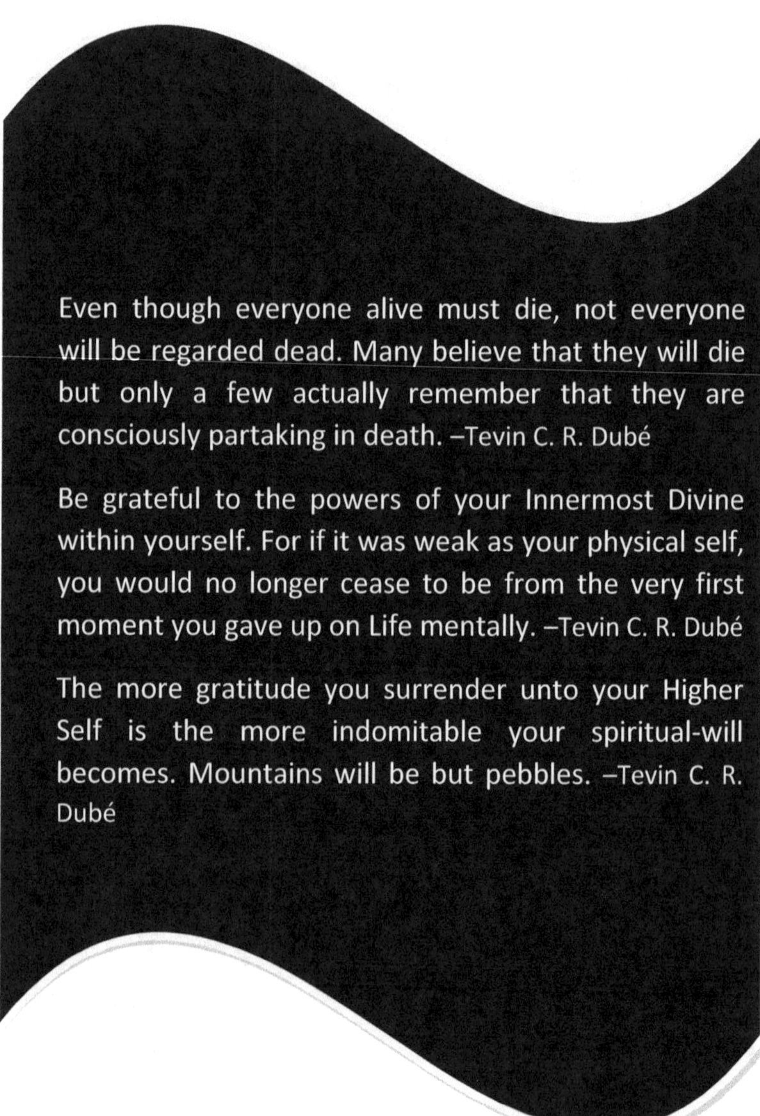

Even though everyone alive must die, not everyone will be regarded dead. Many believe that they will die but only a few actually remember that they are consciously partaking in death. –Tevin C. R. Dubé

Be grateful to the powers of your Innermost Divine within yourself. For if it was weak as your physical self, you would no longer cease to be from the very first moment you gave up on Life mentally. –Tevin C. R. Dubé

The more gratitude you surrender unto your Higher Self is the more indomitable your spiritual-will becomes. Mountains will be but pebbles. –Tevin C. R. Dubé

Great will always be the one who continues to discover and explore that unlimited yet infinite Source that abides within oneself. –Tevin C. R. Dubé

Nature has many tongues and speaks in many languages. Being in Nature will help you to greatly connect to the mysterious nature of that voice within. –Tevin C. R. Dubé

Even silence is a soundless sound because its tone is deafening. Hence it is the best means of communication from your Higher Self. Through various degrees of silence, It yet speaks the loudest. –Tevin C. R. Dubé

To Become requires Becoming. Everything is a process and the beginning of any process requires learning, application, patience, endurance and persistence. –Tevin C. R. Dubé

You are the memory of your ancestors. The more you remember is the greater the entities that once manifested within your lineage shall aid and assist and acknowledge you. You are their remembrance. –Tevin C. R. Dubé

No right thinking mortal will choose mortality over immortality. Remember there is great difference between a human being and being human. –Tevin C. R. Dubé

Upon the final exit, the body may cease to be no more as it breaks back down into the oneness or nothingness of the elements because the Entity within no longer seeks to animate it. You are much more than the body. –Tevin C. R. Dubé

A lot of people are silently learning from you and won't even give you that credit. But nevertheless, it is still a blessing to be a blessing. –Tevin C. R. Dubé

When the Divine open up your eyes to see the things that are not regularly shown, it is the lesser you will speak. –Tevin C. R. Dubé

Alchemise and fashion your life into a positive experience and leave an indelible mark upon all those who are fortunate to experience it both directly and indirectly. –Tevin C. R. Dubé

Many individuals especially the younger generation don't see that their problems has only just begun when the people who genuinely correct them to make better choices is no longer doing such. –Tevin C. R. Dubé

Don't ever take your little knowledge for granted. You'd be surprised to the amount of people who is not in the know as to what you know. –Tevin C. R. Dubé

You can tell when a nation is sick and in a comatose state by extension of its citizens when everything at the end of the day solely revolves and boils down to race, politics and religion. –Tevin C. R. Dubé

The most miserable sets of individuals you will find are the ones who rather focus upon a problem or is either constantly searching or on the lookout for the problem that exists in everything. –Tevin C. R. Dubé

When your emotions overpower you to the point of ingratitude about all the good that was done unto you, you become an ingrate and travesty to yourself. –Tevin C. R. Dubé

If you were to take away the mental influences from institutions such as race, politics and religion a lot of people lives would be meaningless. –Tevin C. R. Dubé

From the moment you realise the elements are alive through their existences, you will never feel lonely the more you connect with them. May the forces always be for you because they are always with you. –Tevin C. R. Dubé

The Great Light of the Divine is that of Carbon and the reflection of it is the release of all the different hues. The darkness we call light and all other colours are but an external glow of this one true ineffable Source. –Tevin C. R. Dubé

The only thing that can shine darkly is Carbon. Even in our perceived sense of light it is ever present in the form of shade. But not only at night it reign but throughout the entire Universe it darkly shines at all times. –Tevin C. R. Dubé

Only ignorance tries to wrong another but wisdom seeks to edify. –Tevin C. R. Dubé

All my quotes and that of others would be useless and worthless unless it is applied. It's like expecting to be clean and not wanting to bathe in the presence of good water and soap. –Tevin C. R. Dubé

There will come a time when many will be required to keep the same energy. As long as your intentions are pure I will say no more. –Tevin C. R. Dubé

This existence called Life is but a test to not only live with, but to overstand, overcome, utilise, incorporate and integrate Fear! It is always here and what you choose to do with it or allow it to do is solely up to you. –Tevin C. R. Dubé

When you realise that you are a projection of the Divine it will make more sense to go within and connect with Source. The ultimate goal is to become One with your Higher Self. –Tevin C. R. Dubé

Every step you take in the direction of becoming a better human being and the best version of yourself is the greater you will naturally display the divinity that has always been ready to be unleashed. –Tevin C. R. Dubé

When you make the ineffable force of love and peace to become great within you, the inheritance of bliss will become an eternal treasure universally bequeathed. –Tevin C. R. Dubé

The best way to honour yourself is to listen and adhere to your own intuition when It speaks. –Tevin C. R. Dubé

Time is in fact a nonentity but yet still to you that is an entity, time is of the essence. –Tevin C. R. Dubé

The greatest and most potent and detrimental of all lock downs is when you lock down your own mind from elevating in consciousness. –Tevin C. R. Dubé

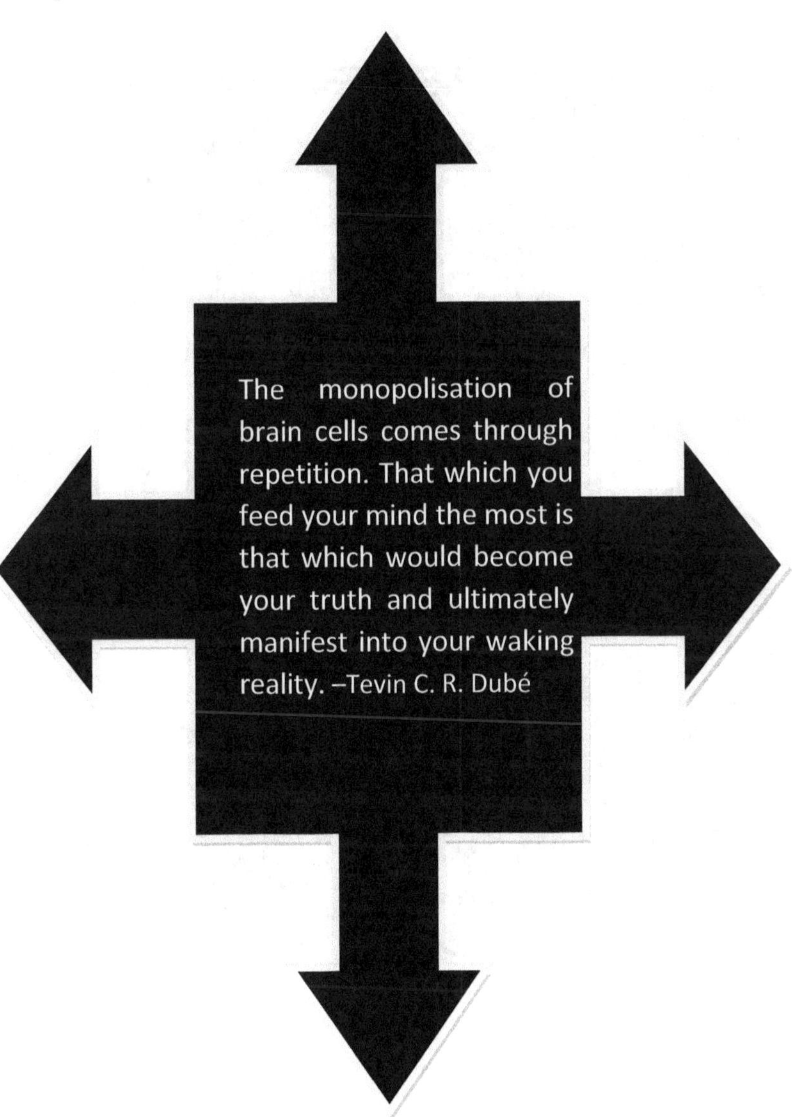
The monopolisation of brain cells comes through repetition. That which you feed your mind the most is that which would become your truth and ultimately manifest into your waking reality. –Tevin C. R. Dubé

The best way to place shackles on the mind is through perpetuating heavy programming over a period of time. Take religion, politics and racism for example. –Tevin C. R. Dubé

The best way to free your mind from any form of bondage and blockage is to always keep an open mind. –Tevin C. R. Dubé

When you learn to set aside your own ignorance, beliefs and concepts and keep an open mind to learning through discourse, reasoning and overstanding, your mind will finally begin to grow its wings. –Tevin C. R. Dubé

Section Two

A lot of you don't even know you could fly all because you don't choose to try and defy gravity. It all begins with the mind. –Tevin C. R. Dubé

A lot of people talk about being free and don't have a real clue about what true freedom looks like. Real freedom is when you finally strip yourself from all desires mortally to just be. –Tevin C. R. Dubé

The bliss about Death is overstanding that there is no such thing as Death. Energy could never die and even though the flesh may perish, the energy that you are already knows that Death is a lie. –Tevin C. R. Dubé

When your desire is no longer to eat solely for taste and recreation but for information; naturally you will begin to resonate with higher vibrations. –Tevin C. R. Dubé

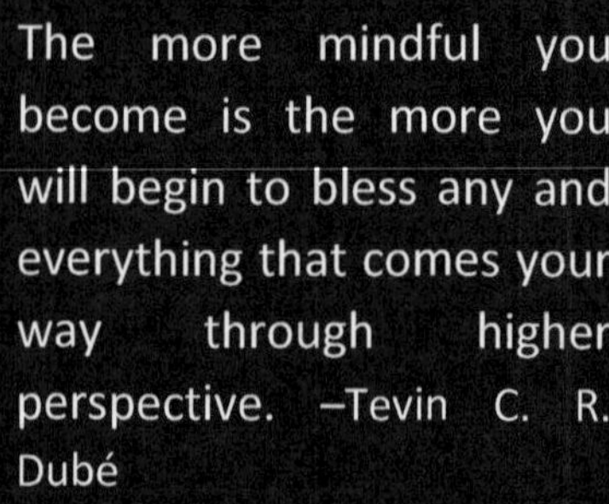

The more mindful you become is the more you will begin to bless any and everything that comes your way through higher perspective. –Tevin C. R. Dubé

Imagination is boundless whereas logic can only happen within boundaries. It is imperative to retain that childlike innocence within. –Tevin C. R. Dubé

Take a look at the impossibility of the entire Universe that is in fact a possibility. What inferior concept makes you to doubt the possibility of the impossible? Anything is possible for the one who ceaselessly believes. –Tevin C. R. Dubé

When you begin to access the Akashic Records or the intelligence of Space, earthbound thinkers will begin to call you crazy even though Earth yet still exists within the intelligence of Space. –Tevin C. R. Dubé

When you learn to rejoice in your down time and with those elevating at the same time, the Universe will reward greatly in divine time. You will see why it wasn't your time. –Tevin C. R. Dubé

Relationships aren't the main validation of your life. Being alive is the ultimate validation of your current existence. Everything else is just an additional bonus that comes with it. There is no need to rush anything. –Tevin C. R. Dubé

Take a good look and see that there is great disadvantage in what many consider as an advantage. And yet there is great advantage in what many may consider as a disadvantage. –Tevin C. R. Dubé

The same way water just flows without any effort is the same way you must allow the knowledge and wisdom of the Universe to flow through you. All you have to do is be open to receive it simply. –Tevin C. R. Dubé

If knowledge is power don't you think it is a wise investment to acquire it! –Tevin C. R. Dubé

The ultimate element of Space is what even holds gravity in place. The very essence of Space is the Supreme Intelligence of the fullness of Absolute Nothingness. –Tevin C. R. Dubé

When you come to truly overstand "Balance" you will from time to time see why everything that is existing was meant to be in existence. Sometimes for peace to continue chaos must ensue. –Tevin C. R. Dubé

The greatest law to be established is to maintain the Order of Balance. –Tevin C. R. Dubé

The reason why my name is attached to all my quotes is because I don't want history to state that the author is unknown. –Tevin C. R. Dubé

All that I am coming to know are the things that I already knew spiritually but momentarily forgot through the incarnation processes of becoming human. –Tevin C. R. Dubé

I am humble enough to admit I am always learning. –Tevin C. R. Dubé

With the increase of healthy mental activities, you will see the need to less speak. Small talk easily becomes a nuisance. –Tevin C. R. Dubé

Idle talkers always find those who rather talk about consciousness, enlightenment and positivity as people who does either talk too much, doesn't make any sense or going crazy. Language barriers! –Tevin C. R. Dubé

An enlightened mind comes to know nothing at all because learning is perpetual. An endarkened mind is one that feels they know it all. –Tevin C. R. Dubé

A true teacher knows they can go the full eight miles with the elaborate explanation of things that they prefer to simply break down in just a few steps. –Tevin C. R. Dubé

Not every teacher of Life actually wants people to innerstand and overstand. A lot prefer the masses to "understand" to the point that they will see the need to remain under. –Tevin C. R. Dubé

Before you make an assumption or form any opinion against someone or something; try to find out the perspectives as to why first. That way you can save yourself from any irrational judgment and the feeling of shame. –Tevin C. R. Dubé

The people who are often fixated upon the negatives will constantly be blinded to answers that are right before their faces. –Tevin C. R. Dubé

Please don't practice the art of putting on a vain expression of personality for the world. In the end you will only make a fool and mockery of yourself. Just be you. –Tevin C. R. Dubé

There is a realm of eternal existence for the identities that were once human consciousness. But in the meantime, those gone will live on in the memories of they who had the opportunity to record them live. –Tevin C. R. Dubé

When you learn to step into the infinite recordings of the Akashic library, not only can you learn but you can also erase and rewrite even memories and thoughts not just of yourself but that of others. –Tevin C. R. Dubé

You are but a minute speck within a speck within the vastness of the element of Space. Yet that small percentage of space that exists within you, once properly accessed, will grant you unlimited access to the All in All. –Tevin C. R. Dubé

Once you can effectively regress into the past without any mental hindrances you can easily be propelled into the future. All of this is possible in the present because they are all simultaneously happening in the Now. –Tevin C. R. Dubé

Being a Saint has nothing to do with being perfect and blemish free. It has everything to do with being a truly genuine soul. –Tevin C. R. Dubé

The qualities and traits of a demon are embodied and expressed in the form of human deception, hypocrisy, a deceitful tongue and treacherous ways; yet fully backed by an envious mind and a heart full of jealousy. –Tevin C. R. Dubé

The thing about demons is that we are in possession of them. The goal is to never allow them to possess you. It's either you learn to master them or allow them to enslave you. –Tevin C. R. Dubé

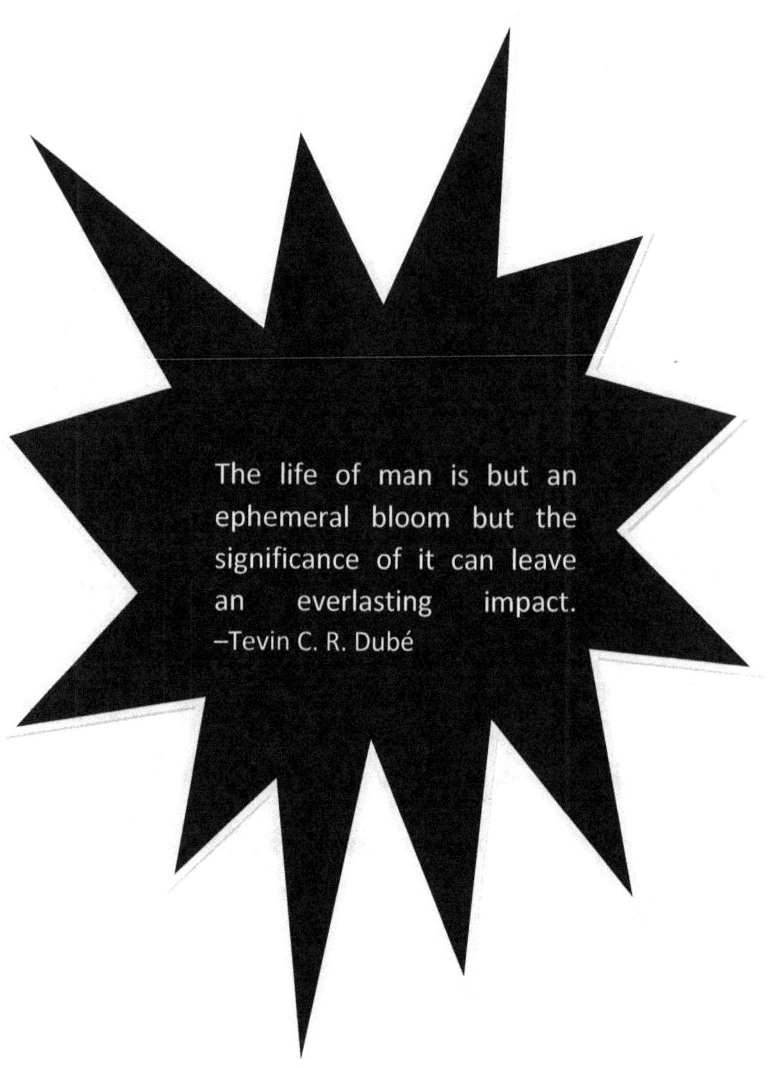
The life of man is but an ephemeral bloom but the significance of it can leave an everlasting impact.
–Tevin C. R. Dubé

Operating out of unabridged love is true strength whereas operating out of pure greed is a weakness of heart. –Tevin C. R. Dubé

One thing about putting your trust in the Universe is that once you push through your own doubts, IT always sends confirmations to encourage your foresight to see beyond the many illusions. –Tevin C. R. Dubé

Being a thinker, many times when I was writing my books, the information that I'd gained, I never came across it before in my entire life. But after I completed them, the proof came in mysterious ways. –Tevin C. R. Dubé

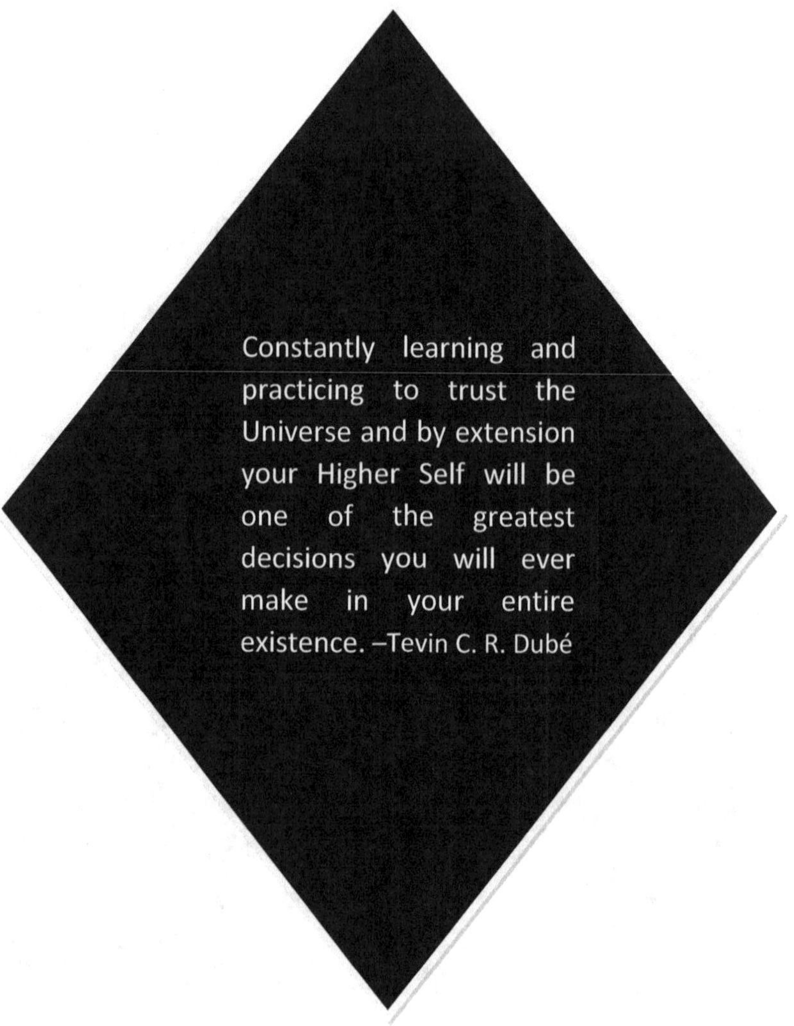
Constantly learning and practicing to trust the Universe and by extension your Higher Self will be one of the greatest decisions you will ever make in your entire existence. –Tevin C. R. Dubé

To trust in the Universe is to move from a state of lack unto the frequencies of abundance. To trust in your Higher Self is to move from a finite state to one that is infinite. –Tevin C. R. Dubé

Always ask for the wisdom to manage the blessings that you are in pursuit to attain. Mismanagement and irresponsibility is what defile your blessings and defeat the true purpose for gaining it. –Tevin C. R. Dubé

The more you learn to become a greater master and ruler within yourself is the more potent your overall frequency, energy and vibration will greatly impact your daily reality. –Tevin C. R. Dubé

It is a rare occurrence for someone to win a battle they are unable to see. Not everything you can always see physically. Many are in turmoil because they are spiritually blind. –Tevin C. R. Dubé

No one has any real evidence of the actual wind itself but the evidence of it takes the form of us as we breathe. It's not so difficult to believe in the divine powers of natural spirituality. –Tevin C. R. Dubé

The rain is but a different version of the sunshine through the processes of precipitation. –Tevin C. R. Dubé

Section Three

He who humbles himself to the wisdom of others will become far much more knowledgeable than the fool filled with ego that always knows. –Tevin C. R. Dubé

Knowledge is the balancing pillar that stands amidst wisdom and overstanding. –Tevin C. R. Dubé

Knowledge is to know. Wisdom comes through the application of what you know. Overstanding comes from the experience of wisdom through the continuous application of what you know. –Tevin C. R. Dubé

The absolute power of The Element of Space is that everything is happening within it but nothing can affect it. Yet everything within is affected by it in one way or another. –Tevin C. R. Dubé

A diamond is formed under immense pressure and after being extracted, the cutting and polishing process can be handled with great ease. Naturally developed toughness exposes true inner beauty of immense worth. –Tevin C. R. Dubé

The ultimate form is to master the state of becoming One with Space. –Tevin C. R. Dubé

The place to hide anything is in plain sight or open space. This is why many have a hard time in locating the Absolute Divine. –Tevin C. R. Dubé

When you learn to roam that void of space within yourself, you will come to literally unearth great power within the dirt of your human self. –Tevin C. R. Dubé

A flower that is in bloom is but a little extension to the overall beauty of the entire plant. –Tevin C. R. Dubé

You and I share but a little space and the best way to honour the Divine is to ensure that you keep it hallowed by spreading a little love here and there. –Tevin C. R. Dubé

Even though there can be a lot of disturbances and movements in any given space; the unperceivable stillness of Space is always undisturbed. –Tevin C. R. Dubé

Only when you effectively learn to become in sync with Space you will be able to affect anything you will. –Tevin C. R. Dubé

The very essence of Space is the ultimate recording system and Intelligent Observer of all things. –Tevin C. R. Dubé

All trees, plants and bushes are fruitful. If not with fruit, they are full with healing, but overall fruitful when it comes to the replenishing of oxygen. –Tevin C. R. Dubé

It takes only one person to appreciate the value of you that will change the entire landscape of the demand of you. Not everyone is worthy though. –Tevin C. R. Dubé

The same way a moth is attracted to flames is in the same manner small-minded individuals are attracted to stupidity. In the end, they both get burned to a crisp. – Tevin C. R. Dubé

It is most easy for the human mind to delve into the understanding of dynamic matters but most difficult to comprehend the complex nature and overstanding of simplicity. – Tevin C. R. Dubé

To the rare few of us that had major near death experience(s); death was never the intention. The epiphanies and awakenings were. – Tevin C. R. Dubé

When you finally awaken to the truth to that which is actually looking through the windows of your soul, the game is over as soon as it begins. –Tevin C. R. Dubé

One of the greatest misconceptions is that your eyes can see. The eyes are but a medium or a peephole for that which is existing and looking from beyond. –Tevin C. R. Dubé

If you continue to remain optimistic and amplify your positive energies in times of negativity; when that time inevitably comes to an end, you will be an even greater force to be reckoned with. –Tevin C. R. Dubé

When you first learn to confront, conquer and subdue the ugly that is within you, then the true beauty about yourself will naturally flow from the inside-out. –Tevin C. R. Dubé

Your greatest disappointment can reveal the ugliest side that you never knew existed in the dark. But it can also reveal strength, courage and willpower you never knew you had that existed in the light of that darkness. –Tevin C. R. Dubé

Don't only follow your dreams but allow it to take you to the places where you are meant to be. Don't only follow your dreams but allow it to take you to your purpose. –Tevin C. R. Dubé

Imagination/Visualisation of that which you wish to manifest is the commencement of the procreation process with the Universe. Self-doubt, lack of confidence and belief are the means of abortion. –Tevin C. R. Dubé

Death is an opportunity that can either instill gratitude in you or reveal how grateful you were or how much of an ungrateful person you have been. Overall, Death is still an opportunity in more ways than one. –Tevin C. R. Dubé

When you reject Knowledge, you will become a pupil of Fear. –Tevin C. R. Dubé

Fear could never strip you of your power; it only makes you to use it against yourself. –Tevin C. R. Dubé

The most insane man in the world is one that is seeing but is yet still following the lead from he that is blind. –Tevin C. R. Dubé

The most dangerous leader in the world is the one who is driven by the hunger for money and power. Such a one will both sell and devour their own. –Tevin C. R. Dubé

Education; even though it can assist a little is not the remedy to cure and heal stupidity. Common sense and being able to think is and not just the ability to memorise stuff well. –Tevin C. R. Dubé

A nation that is devoid of common sense is one that is full of zombies and headless chickens. –Tevin C. R. Dubé

Trick or Treat? The treats in the physical is actually the trick because it is ever so temporal but very present yet the treats of the spiritual are eternal but the trick is to see beyond the physical illusion of its absence. –Tevin C. R. Dubé

I agree that Life is a test even a gauntlet for some of us but with pure will and determination; your story in overcoming is the true glory. –Tevin C. R. Dubé

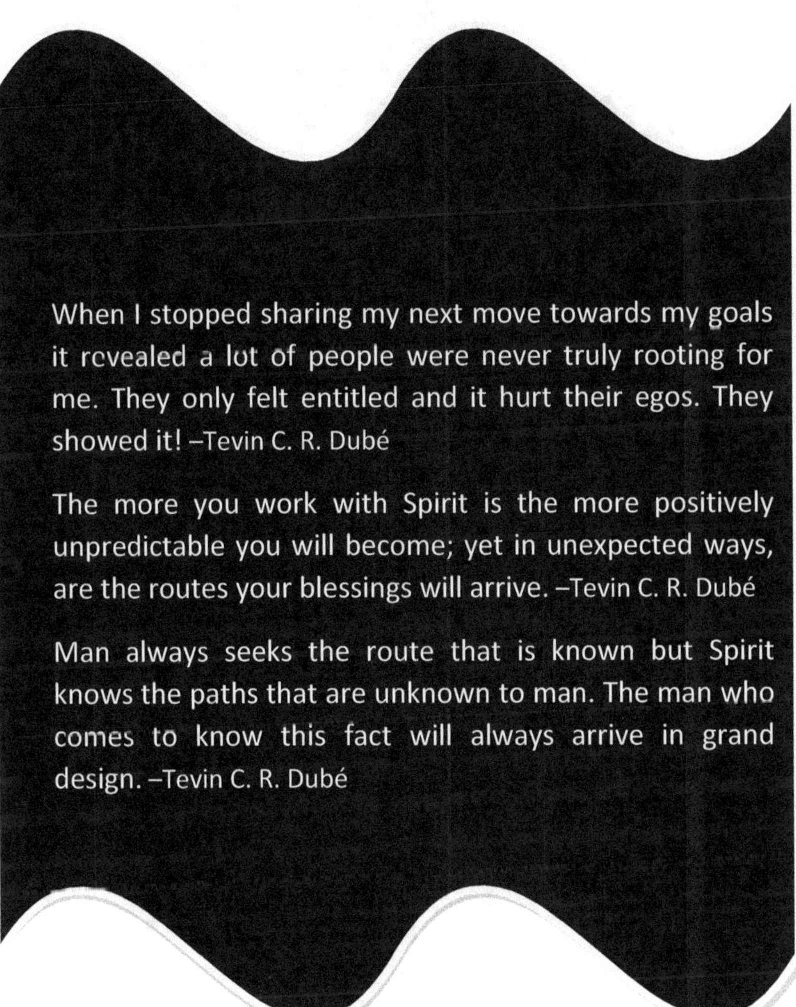

When I stopped sharing my next move towards my goals it revealed a lot of people were never truly rooting for me. They only felt entitled and it hurt their egos. They showed it! –Tevin C. R. Dubé

The more you work with Spirit is the more positively unpredictable you will become; yet in unexpected ways, are the routes your blessings will arrive. –Tevin C. R. Dubé

Man always seeks the route that is known but Spirit knows the paths that are unknown to man. The man who comes to know this fact will always arrive in grand design. –Tevin C. R. Dubé

There is walking, jogging, running, catching a taxi, taking a boat ride, catching a flight; all logic to get from point A to point B, yet in the spirit you can leap timelines in a split second. –Tevin C. R. Dubé

What is mandated in the physical can be liberated in the spiritual. Not everything that goes up must come back down. And not everything that goes around must come back around. –Tevin C. R. Dubé

Silence is the easiest language to learn yet the most difficult thing to speak when you don't learn to take full control of your own tongue. –Tevin C. R. Dubé

The true problem begins the more you eat for taste and recreation and not Life and information. –Tevin C. R. Dubé

Navel healthcare is of utmost importance too. That is not just your link to your mother but also the source connection to all the ancestral mothers that came before her. –Tevin C. R. Dubé

When meditating it is good to incorporate the elements because whether you are conscious of it or not they are an integral part of our existence. Therefore, it is good to greatly acknowledge them. –Tevin C. R. Dubé

Each and every one of us has dirty/dutty ways. But the real problem is when you don't learn to see it, accept it, and at least try to fix it for yourself. –Tevin C. R. Dubé

Those who barely find time to fix themselves are often times pointing their finger and wasting their precious time judging others. –Tevin C. R. Dubé

If not anything, the one thing I found to be common is that the ones who love to judge others the most hates to be judged by others the most. Do so, don't like so. –Tevin C. R. Dubé

There is a difference between critiquing and criticism. There is also a great difference between constructive criticism and being embarrassing. –Tevin C. R. Dubé

In more ways than one a judger masters the ability to fix the lives of others greater than they can even fix their own. –Tevin C. R. Dubé

It becomes such a great disappointment and shame when the judger that once knew it all must accept their wrongs when the one they judged begins to do much better than they had anticipated and predicted. –Tevin C. R. Dubé

It pays greatly to be humble. That way, when you have nothing good to say, you are humble enough to know when to keep certain things to yourself. –Tevin C. R. Dubé

The more you focus upon others opinions of you and what they say is the least attention you will pay towards the further development of yourself. Don't do yourself the same injustice that they are doing unto themselves. –Tevin C. R. Dubé

When you put on clothes it moves with you but your clothes aren't alive. It is the same thing with your body; it is never alive but the real you are the one wearing it as clothes. –Tevin C. R. Dubé

When you effectively learn to incorporate your intuition with intellect; this union of the subconscious and logic will grant you a mind that is limitless. –Tevin C. R. Dubé

Section Four

Many are older than others by age in this generation but few, even though younger, are older than most by generations. The evidence is made clear through the natural possession of knowledge and wisdom. –Tevin C. R. Dubé

Most are working on solely becoming powerful in Earth's temporal existence but few are also working on becoming powerful in the spiritual realm that is eternal. A man here but a God there. –Tevin C. R. Dubé

If you want to gain true power seek spirituality and find a new way to establish and implement it physically. Either way, spiritual inheritance is eternal forevermore. –Tevin C. R. Dubé

The initial scientific fact is that a truly natural healthy lifestyle is the idealistic gift one can give to their body. A lot of people are simply just too lazy and indiscipline to truly love themselves so they mostly rely on synthetic means, idiocy, and ignorance to continue the practice of their own self-hate and use statements like, "I didn't come here to turn stone." While this may be true it is still your choice to either live unto death or suffer unto it. Moderation is the key to any form of longevity. Through knowledge, wisdom and careful observation it is very clear to see.
–Tevin C. R. Dubé

When your aura or bioelectrical field is damaged or weakened, you are not only more susceptible to take on damage from spiritual attacks but risk getting physically sick as a result of an unhealthy immune system. –Tevin C. R. Dubé

The man who learns how to effectively channel both his feelings of creation and natural emotions can make universal shifts from within through the spiritual body to alter reality. –Tevin C. R. Dubé

Your aura/bioelectrical field are in fact your spiritual shield. To maintain that shield requires healthy eating and positive thinking. The more you enhance it, the greater you can feel your own energy surrounding you. –Tevin C. R. Dubé

You could never compare someone who is solely brilliant in academics to someone who is brilliant enough to add up the mathematics of Life. –Tevin C. R. Dubé

We don't need any more academically qualified individuals to run a nation. We need people who are also versatile in memorising the book of Nature and know how to read that which is within. –Tevin C. R. Dubé

Any system that doesn't incorporate Life and Truth as its source of operation; lies, suffering and death will always be the end results. –Tevin C. R. Dubé

The beginning of the age of ignorance, self-destruction, totalitarian measures and any form of oppression and enslavement either mentally or physically begins from the moment spirituality is rejected. –Tevin C. R. Dubé

Your body is likened unto a lamp and within it, is the temporal home to a great Genie. From the moment you learn to summon It, your wish is your command. –Tevin C. R. Dubé

Light could never reveal Darkness because it is in fact the Darkness that reveals the intensity of Light. –Tevin C. R. Dubé

When you learn to become the light within your darkness, it becomes easier for you to maneuver yourself through the eternal nature and vastness of darkness. Light is yet still a part of the Dark. –Tevin C. R. Dubé

Life is always alive. –Tevin C. R. Dubé

The moment you stop differentiating between what you consider to be good or bad without thorough overstanding is when you will arrive at a state of mental equilibrium. –Tevin C. R. Dubé

I don't ever truly consider myself as a good person and because of such; I don't project others to be truly bad. To be human is to be on a level field with everyone else that is still alive. –Tevin C. R. Dubé

The good is always at war with the bad. But even though this endless war rages on, both the good and bad is always at peace with Balance. –Tevin C. R. Dubé

A vision will always be greater than a desire. Desires can change at any time because it is personal but a vision includes a bigger picture than yourself because it wishes to include many others. –Tevin C. R. Dubé

Life is a dream all of us are destined to awaken from.

Whenever your emotions get in control of you, you not only become a threat to others but a greater danger unto yourself. –Tevin C. R. Dubé

From the moment you give control over to the things you ought to be in control of is exactly when the inception of catastrophe has only just begun. –Tevin C. R. Dubé

The same way your stomach has a natural appetite to be fed is the same with your spirit that must be fueled, nourished and fed with the Knowledge of Self. –Tevin C. R. Dubé

Don't be a human that only knows how to quench the thirst of the flesh and not the spirit. That will only lead to vexation of spirit and a fixed bitterness of heart. –Tevin C. R. Dubé

When you go to bathe you don't leave out your hands or feet. So when you cleansing your entire body make sure to take time to also clean up your heart and mind. –Tevin C. R. Dubé

Games have taught me something valuable about Life. Even though some stages are hard just keep "Playing" and eventually you will beat it. –Tevin C. R. Dubé

Whenever you find yourself in a position where someone is treating you as competition, take your time and stride. No matter how far they run ahead, always remember that you are initially the race. –Tevin C. R. Dubé

Carbon/Darkness is the greatest Light because it is the only thing you can make out without actually making out exactly what it is. –Tevin C. R. Dubé

Reading books will definitely enhance your mind but learning to read that universal book within your soul will definitely enhance you spiritually and beyond. –Tevin C. R. Dubé

Not every perceived blessing is a blessing and not every perceived curse is a curse. Higher perspective will easily help you to establish this fact. –Tevin C. R. Dubé

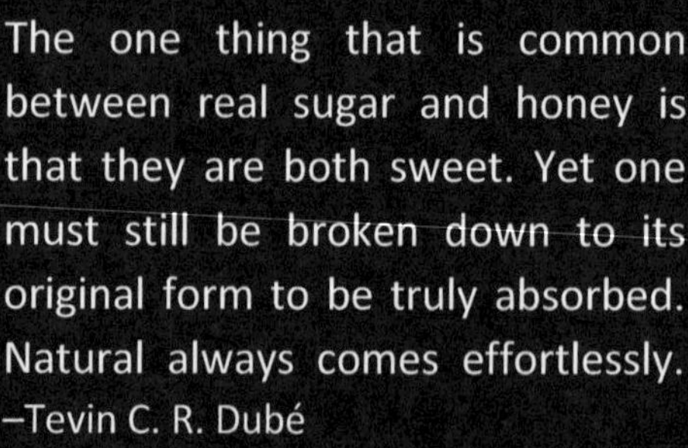

The one thing that is common between real sugar and honey is that they are both sweet. Yet one must still be broken down to its original form to be truly absorbed. Natural always comes effortlessly. –Tevin C. R. Dubé

Many don't realise how contagious stupidity and naivety really is until they have either stumbled across knowledge or adhered to inherited wisdom. –Tevin C. R. Dubé

The more you learn to find yourself is the less you will operate out of imbalanced emotions. –Tevin C. R. Dubé

Always remember when you are accomplishing greatness, the silence or lack of support doesn't mean that you aren't being noticed. The Universe always demonstrates Its greatness by showing and proving. –Tevin C. R. Dubé

Always think highly of yourself but never to the point where your ego is the one in full control. –Tevin C. R. Dubé

There are different levels to either being just or unjust. Yet without balance both can prove to be very chaotic where the concept of justice and injustice are concerned. –Tevin C. R. Dubé

Complexity in its truest form is likened unto the appearance of a mirage that prefers to take on the form of simplicity. –Tevin C. R. Dubé

A lot of things seem to be impossible for may in this world because they are not in tuned spiritually or making themselves familiar with the spiritual realms. –Tevin C. R. Dubé

If a nation has been practicing a naturally proper health regiment for over an extended period of time prior, that nation would never have any worries about this pandemic. –Tevin C. R. Dubé

On a positive to negative and vice versa relationship about Covid-19; even though many have succumbed to it many more lives have been spared from accidents, drowning and other casualties. But with Life comes Death. –Tevin C. R. Dubé

The ignorant in mind and ways will often times have to repeat the same lesson over and over again. –Tevin C. R. Dubé

To be ignorant in the face of facts will always leave you in a remedial state in Life. –Tevin C. R. Dubé

Whenever you are looking for a true partnership look for someone who truly loves their self the way you love yourself. Stop looking for people to put work into who doesn't put in the work themselves. –Tevin C. R. Dubé

Imagine you can feel the sun's energy touching you even though it isn't really touching you. If that isn't magical enough for you to perceive then you will miss a lot of magical stuff about your own being. –Tevin C. R. Dubé

The wise knows that physical strength is always secondary to spiritual strength. Only the fool chooses to interfere with any and everybody. Never underestimate or take simplicity for stupidity. –Tevin C. R. Dubé

One thing is common with those who dare to accomplish the impossible and bring it to fruition. Their source of strength always comes from within and is beyond this world. That is the work of the spirit. –Tevin C. R. Dubé

The Spirit is like the director behind the movie scene. It already knows the direction of the film. Allow it to guide you and make additions or cuts and watch your life become an epic masterpiece. –Tevin C. R. Dubé

The more you work with the spiritual is the more the spiritual will conspire with you. So the more you become in tune with Spirit is the more Spirit becomes in tune with you. The goal is to always attain Oneness. –Tevin C. R. Dubé

The most dynamic form of anything is humbled by great simplicity. –Tevin C. R. Dubé

Remove the pans upon either side of a scale and you will still be left with the pillar standing firmly in the middle. Without that initial establishment of balance the scales could never work. –Tevin C. R. Dubé

Do not confine your ability to learn solely through academics because it is just a tiny aspect within the vastness of Life. Don't just aspire to be filled with words and be devoid of Life itself. –Tevin C. R. Dubé

The Source Energy that you have within you already possesses the power to make possible the impossible. Learn to connect with IT by becoming a conduit to effectively channel IT. The key is to believe in yourself. –Tevin C. R. Dubé

Section Five

The more you grow is the more you will be overstood by those who have grown but greatly misunderstood by those who either stunt their own growth or just don't want to grow. –Tevin C. R. Dubé

The mind of a pessimist is much messier than the aftermath left in the wake of a natural disaster. –Tevin C. R. Dubé

When you don't learn to make yourself approve, just like a cheater in an exam; you rob yourself from developing your mental capacity. –Tevin C. R. Dubé

When you are not in alignment with the Universe you will experience both high and low voltage in your energy body which ultimately affects the mind. Alignment equates to Balance. –Tevin C. R. Dubé

We all are walking together on the road of Life but everyone is still trekking upon their own individual path. Only the few that are focused can actually see this. –Tevin C. R. Dubé

We are the most natural form of magnets. You can tell whether the energy of others is compatible or repelling to you naturally without thought. Yet many betray themselves when their mind suggests otherwise. –Tevin C. R. Dubé

The more you see things from a negative perspective, the more bitterness will spring ceaselessly from within your heart, mind and soul. –Tevin C. R. Dubé

The same way you can become possessed by lower vibrational beings when you lower your vibrations is the same way you can possess higher vibrational beings when you increase your vibrations. –Tevin C. R. Dubé

The more you learn to master your energies, even though they are somewhat possessing you, is the greater you will literally possess them in that they will always obey your every command. –Tevin C. R. Dubé

The same way spirits can possess a human physically is the same way a human can possess a spirit spiritually. All you need to do is to overstand the functions of energy. –Tevin C. R. Dubé

To become awakened is to be like a newborn unto the entire Universe. It realigns and repositions Itself just to accommodate you. It becomes highly overprotective of you. –Tevin C. R. Dubé

It is very easy to tell when someone has no timing or is offbeat. Those awkward feeling moments, insecurities, depression and other mental imbalances are signs that you are not in sync spiritually with the Source within. –Tevin C. R. Dubé

Always remember you could never truly loss something you never really had. It only feels like a loss because you thought you had it in the first place. –Tevin C. R. Dubé

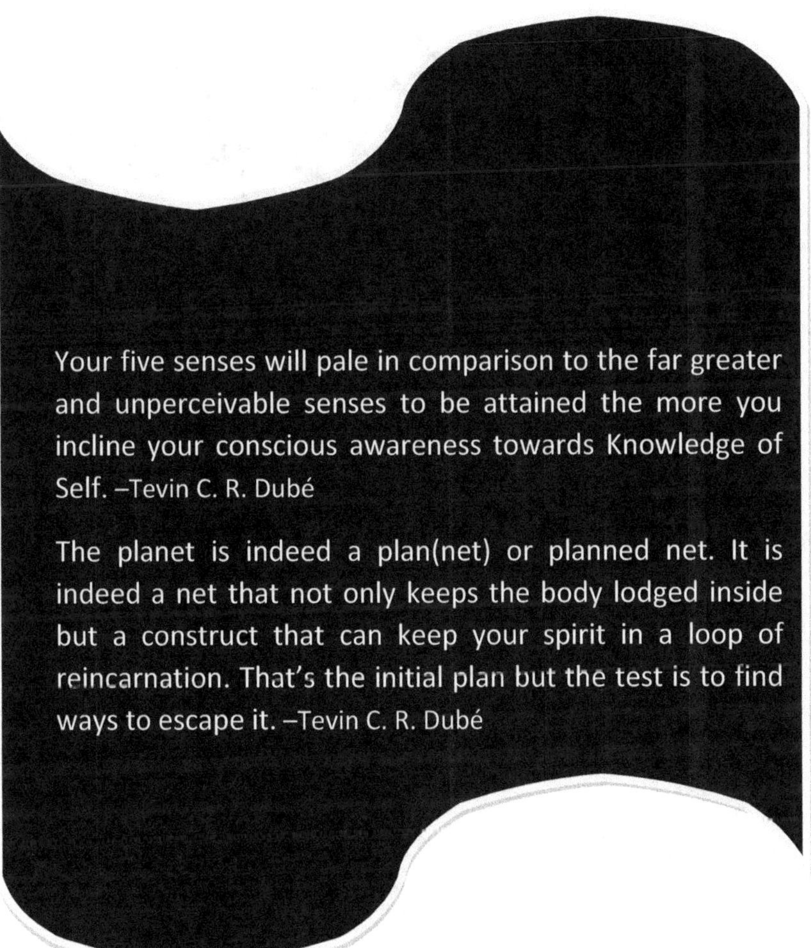

Your five senses will pale in comparison to the far greater and unperceivable senses to be attained the more you incline your conscious awareness towards Knowledge of Self. –Tevin C. R. Dubé

The planet is indeed a plan(net) or planned net. It is indeed a net that not only keeps the body lodged inside but a construct that can keep your spirit in a loop of reincarnation. That's the initial plan but the test is to find ways to escape it. –Tevin C. R. Dubé

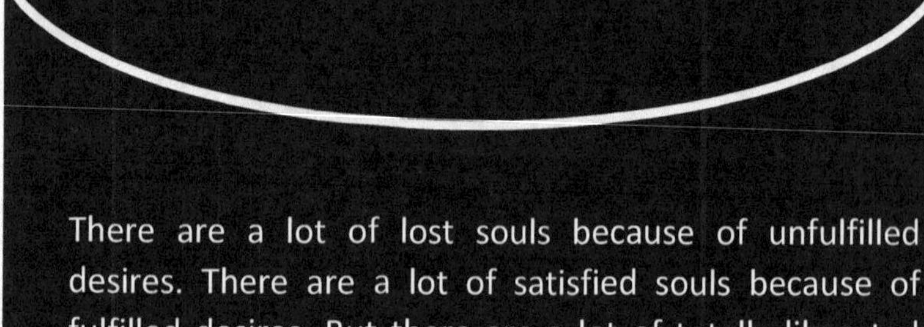

There are a lot of lost souls because of unfulfilled desires. There are a lot of satisfied souls because of fulfilled desires. But there are a lot of totally liberated souls because they no longer have any desire to desire. –Tevin C. R. Dubé

The strongest man in the world is not he who has the most physical strength but he who has learned to master the uncontrollable might of his subconscious mind. –Tevin C. R. Dubé

A bird after it passes its initial threshold of growth intuitively knows it possesses the ability to fly. Point is, your intuition naturally knows your fullest capabilities. Learn to fully trust and believe it. –Tevin C. R. Dubé

A fish trusts in its ability to swim, a bird trusts in its wings ability to fly, a dog trusts in its ability to smell. This trust comes natural. As a human, your intuition comes naturally so beware of your second thought. –Tevin C. R. Dubé

There is a conscious form of insanity rampant in the Earth. Many know about the madness of others and are yet unaware of their own. –Tevin C. R. Dubé

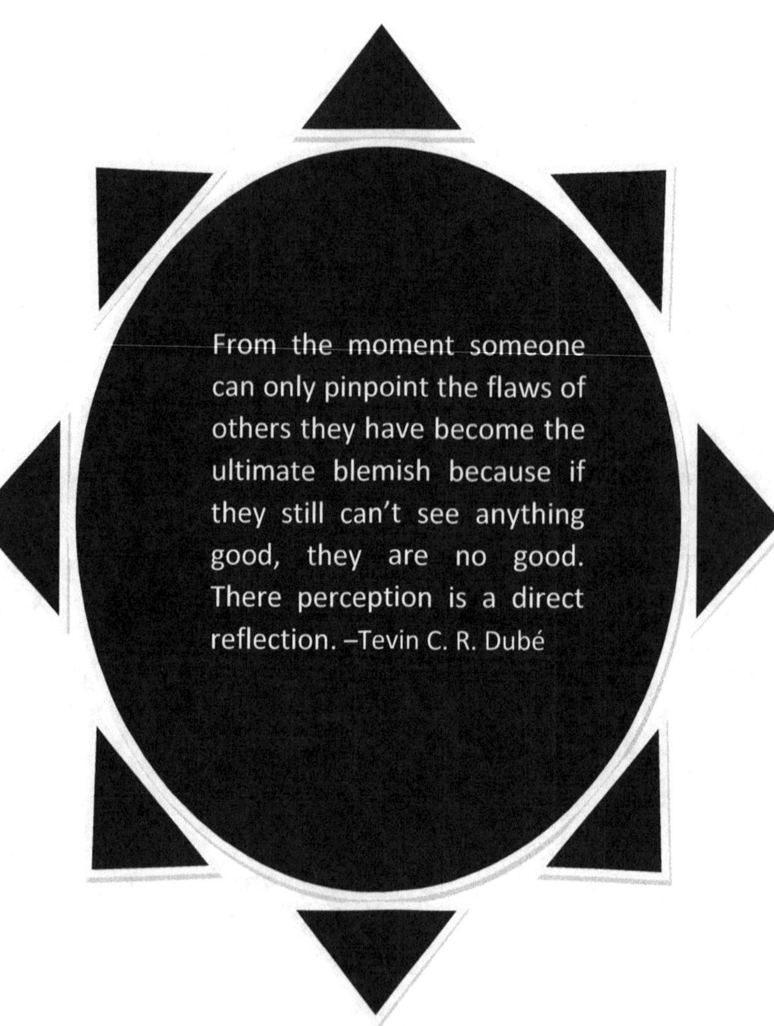
From the moment someone can only pinpoint the flaws of others they have become the ultimate blemish because if they still can't see anything good, they are no good. There perception is a direct reflection. –Tevin C. R. Dubé

Light and Dark is not always indicative of good and evil. Take for instance day and night or heat and shade. Each serves its purpose unto the maintenance of Balance. –Tevin C. R. Dubé

A demon is but a low vibrational being. To be affected by them you must lower your vibration. To fear them is to lower your vibration. To become like one you must lower your vibration. –Tevin C. R. Dubé

Genuinely support others. Don't just support people with the silent intention to be supported in return. When it's your turn your support will be unfathomable because the Universe loves to reward a genuine heart, mind and soul. –Tevin C. R. Dubé

One thing about a deceitful man is that his own tongue beats him badly. –Tevin C. R. Dubé

One thing I've come to innerstand is that the human intellect cannot be compared nor compete with the source intelligence of intuition. It is literally impossible. –Tevin C. R. Dubé

Sometimes the Universe tests your greatest beliefs. And more than ever, a lot of people tend to fail themselves during the process. –Tevin C. R. Dubé

There are those who will reach a regular height in Life once thought impossible and be filled with ego. Then there are those who will come to humbly show them that their once impossible height is but a bump in a flat plain. –Tevin C. R. Dubé

Some people will always just do it for the money. They will toss aside their integrity because of feigned lips and a deceitful heart. –Tevin C. R. Dubé

The same way the upholder is worse than the thief is in the same manner for a man that goes against his own word. A man who is easy to betray himself will even deceive those closest to his heart. –Tevin C. R. Dubé

In my lucid dream state one night, Source expressed greatly from within how much IT loathes deceitfulness. –Tevin C. R. Dubé

Sometimes your table must remain empty but for a while as the table of another close by gets served. That way, the loafers, hopers and mocking pretenders will expose themselves. The Universe is never late. –Tevin C. R. Dubé

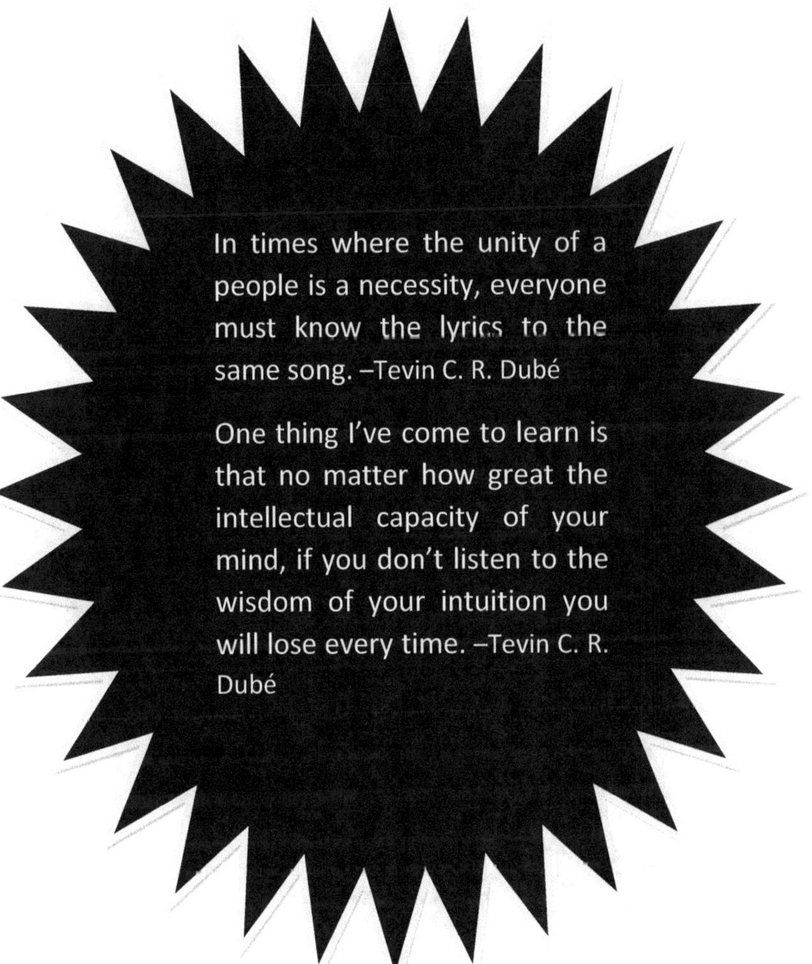
In times where the unity of a people is a necessity, everyone must know the lyrics to the same song. –Tevin C. R. Dubé

One thing I've come to learn is that no matter how great the intellectual capacity of your mind, if you don't listen to the wisdom of your intuition you will lose every time. –Tevin C. R. Dubé

He who loves to play blind to the truth will easily be destroyed by lies. A word to the wise. –Tevin C. R. Dubé

Don't ever get caught up in the fear of those who will do just about anything because they have to sing for their supper. –Tevin C. R. Dubé

One of the saddest lives to live is the one where someone just chooses to mind everyone else business instead of investing that time into the quality of their own. –Tevin C. R. Dubé

When you remain true to yourself, express sincere genuineness, observe and pay close attention; you will clearly see the extent of the envy and jealousy of many. –Tevin C. R. Dubé

The best way to genuinely express your love is to infinity and beyond. That way, your essence will know no bounds. –Tevin C. R. Dubé

I AM THAT I AM. I AM WHO I AM. I WILL WHO I AM. FOREVER I AM. I AM FOREVER. I AM ETERNAL. –Tevin C. R. Dubé

When you work with the spiritual you will see many things the regular eyes cannot perceive. –Tevin C. R. Dubé

Majority of the people who want things to go back to normal are more concerned with making money than bettering humanity. –Tevin C. R. Dubé

Even in a lie a little truth must be incorporated to make it seem realistic. Be mindful of those who only trying to pass of everything that is not in alignment to their thesis as false information. –Tevin C. R. Dubé

Section Six

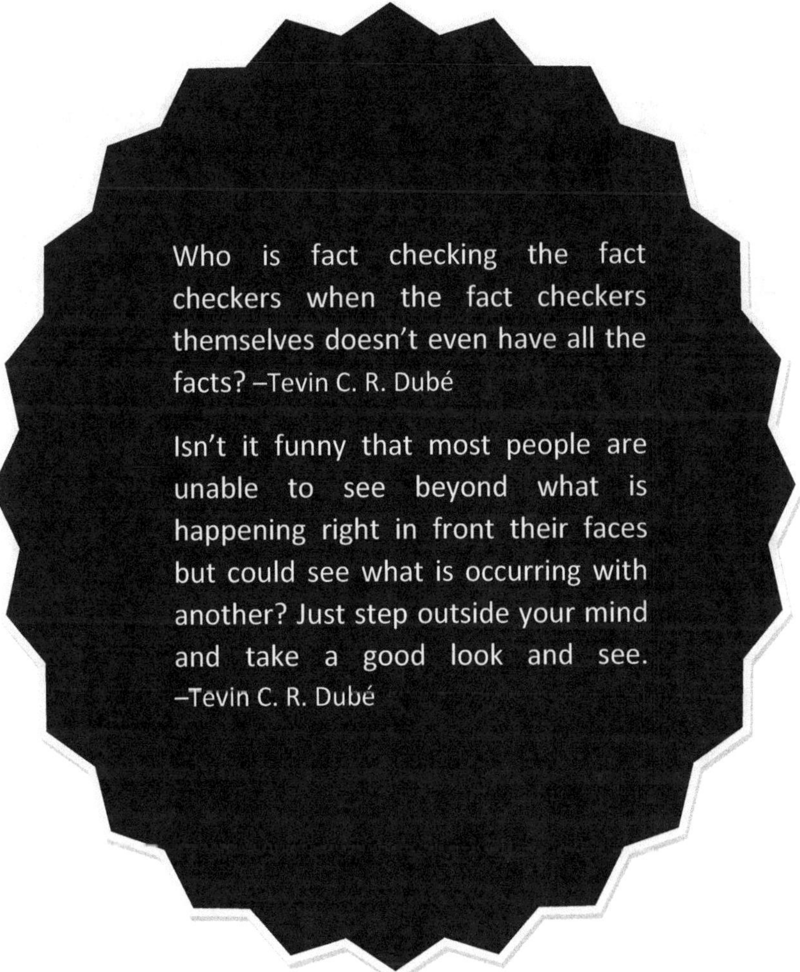
Who is fact checking the fact checkers when the fact checkers themselves doesn't even have all the facts? –Tevin C. R. Dubé

Isn't it funny that most people are unable to see beyond what is happening right in front their faces but could see what is occurring with another? Just step outside your mind and take a good look and see. –Tevin C. R. Dubé

The person standing outside the game of chest always sees the moves clearer. The world is playing a game of chess and many can't even see that they are pawns. –Tevin C. R. Dubé

All the smart fools who are only seeking to protect their financial investments and interests are too smart to even see that one day, they too will die and leave it all behind. –Tevin C. R. Dubé

The worst kind of leader you can inherit is one who can only guide you physically but spiritually leave you lost in a perpetual labyrinth. –Tevin C. R. Dubé

The shepherd will always exploit the sheep. If he doesn't harvest the fleece, he will sell some alive and some in parts, and others he himself will digest along the way. –Tevin C. R. Dubé

Imagine if a man will betray his own for silver what will he do if gold is presented before him. –Tevin C. R. Dubé

A leader that could easily be misled will be the detriment to those whom is led. –Tevin C. R. Dubé

Someone can be chosen but never appointed as much as someone that has been appointed was never chosen. Only time and circumstances will make this clear. –Tevin C. R. Dubé

How would you feel about someone making a decision for you without your involvement? You won't like it so then how are many of you taking it so easy? –Tevin C. R. Dubé

The best way to train your immune system is with what you choose to ingest. To do it naturally you need to consume that which is natural otherwise you will need artificial training to combat artificial eating and drinking. –Tevin C. R. Dubé

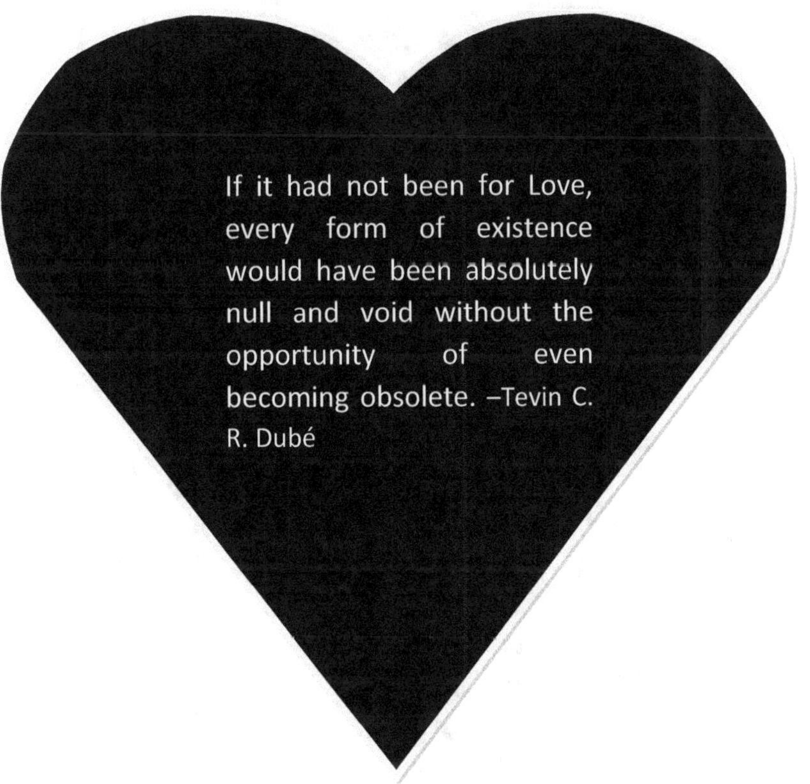
If it had not been for Love, every form of existence would have been absolutely null and void without the opportunity of even becoming obsolete. –Tevin C. R. Dubé

If you hear herbs are the healing of a nation and marijuana alone comes to mind, you have been mentally programmed. –Tevin C. R. Dubé

Those who are too concerned about going back to a world that was never normal are the ones who are too distracted to see that normalcy never existed. The proof is in the pudding or the pandemic should I say? –Tevin C. R. Dubé

Above everything, seeking knowledge and learning to question everything is not just a biblical fact but a fundamental principle that is universal towards your livelihood and survival. –Tevin C. R. Dubé

The way the mind works it could either be your best friend or your own worst enemy if you don't take control of it. Fear has made many betray themselves and led to some even killing themselves and not knowing such. –Tevin C. R. Dubé

The conditioning of mind was fundamental for the oppression of slavery to work. Take some time to see how much mind conditioning has and is still taking place during this worldwide pandemic season.
—Tevin C. R. Dubé

The house Nigger is always the most treacherous one upon the plantation because of his closeness to massa. A slave that doesn't acknowledge their enslavement is a bringer of generational curses.
—Tevin C. R. Dubé

When you don't learn to digest the truth, you will starve from lies. –Tevin C. R. Dubé

The same way a hibernating bear must wake up or risk dying from hunger is the same humanity will have to rise or risk dying from hunger for the truth. –Tevin C. R. Dubé

Only sometimes you must go with the flow but not every time. Only a dead fish does that. –Tevin C. R. Dubé

All the people who are trying to quiet and oppress those who are speaking truth will soon have a terrible fate to meet in this Life from and by The Divine who sent those messages personally. –Tevin C. R. Dubé

The real fight that is taking place is way bigger than you think. These little governments are just the first line of defence. –Tevin C. R. Dubé

You could never make money off a healthy person but from human error, naivety, stupidity and overall lack of knowledge. –Tevin C. R. Dubé

I am yet to see a medical professional on our major media platforms as the helm of our country endorsing healthy lifestyle practices other than taking the vaccine. –Tevin C. R. Dubé

Places like America where there is an abundance of concrete, junk foods, drugs, lack of fresh air, natural herbs and vegetation will always have a higher mortality rate when any virus spreads. –Tevin C. R. Dubé

No matter how much the truth is sunk or buried it will always rise to the surface bigger, better and stronger. –Tevin C. R. Dubé

Make true knowledge mandatory. Make good agriculture without the usage of chemical growth enhancements mandatory. Make healthy eating and drinking mandatory. –Tevin C. R. Dubé

You could never ask for freedom and obtain it once captured. You must take it and to do such you have to fight for it because the one doing the capturing has every intention to keep it that way. —Tevin C. R. Dubé

A people that don't learn to speak up as one will continue to babble amongst themselves individually. U.N.I.T.Y. Unity is both the beginning and the end to the most complex of situations. —Tevin C. R. Dubé

A public disclaimer: Politicians are not Scientists. —Tevin C. R. Dubé

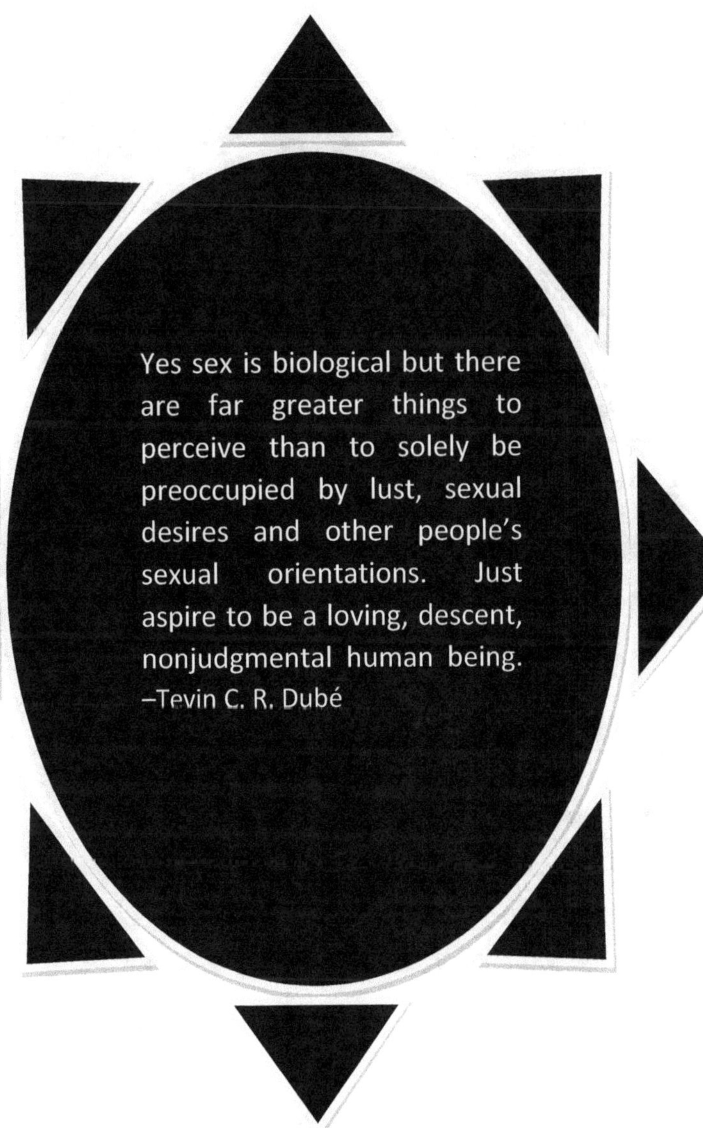
Yes sex is biological but there are far greater things to perceive than to solely be preoccupied by lust, sexual desires and other people's sexual orientations. Just aspire to be a loving, descent, nonjudgmental human being.
—Tevin C. R. Dubé

You won't believe the amount of things that doesn't bother you after you die. So do yourself a favour by trying to not worry too much, if not at all. Don't die while you're still alive.
—Tevin C. R. Dubé

The irony about the concept of Life and Death is that Life is a death sentence and Death is a life sentence.
—Tevin C. R. Dubé

For every action there is a reaction. Learning how to not react is still a reaction. This reaction-less reaction is in fact the ultimate form of reaction.
—Tevin C. R. Dubé

In the physical sense you cannot affect a spirit as much a spirit cannot affect you. But on an energetic level where frequency and vibration are concerned both can and do affect each other. –Tevin C. R. Dubé

Intuition is always right but human intellect always begs to differ. Intuition enlightens then steps back and watch you make a fool of yourself and then say, "You see!" It has nothing to prove but is always willing to guide you truthfully. –Tevin C. R. Dubé

The nature of the carnal man despite his own shortcomings in Life would still prefer another that errs just like himself to suffer perpetually for it but seek pardon for himself. The Devil is alive. –Tevin C. R. Dubé

Don't go walking into a lion's den and expect not to be eaten. –Tevin C. R. Dubé

We are all consumers in Life. Some consume wildlife and livestock but there are those who seek to devour human life. Human energy is Earth's most precious commodity. –Tevin C. R. Dubé

Some of the purest things we need for our survival are tasteless; like water and oxygen. Not everything that tastes good means you good. –Tevin C. R. Dubé

It is such a shame that a people who came directly from Nature are yet to learn at least one of the many voices of It. To not to be aware of Nature is to not be aware of yourself. –Tevin C. R. Dubé

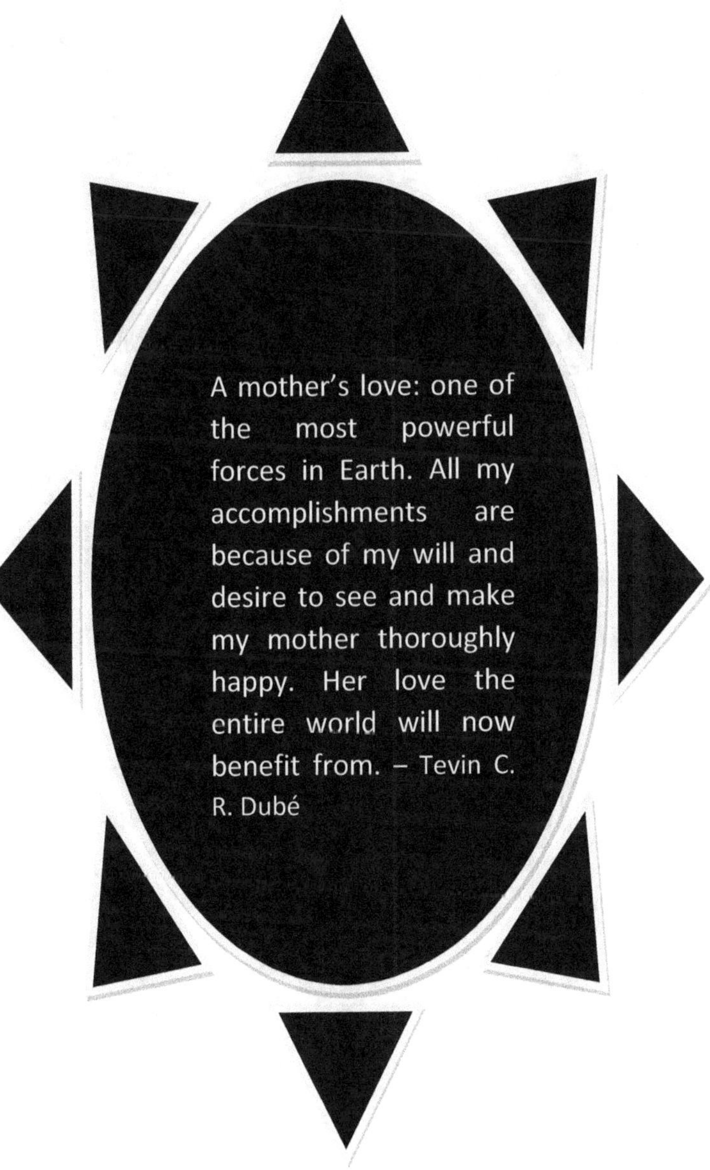
A mother's love: one of the most powerful forces in Earth. All my accomplishments are because of my will and desire to see and make my mother thoroughly happy. Her love the entire world will now benefit from. – Tevin C. R. Dubé

The wise always empties himself to the fact that he doesn't pretend or claim to know everything but the fool always remains full with the pretentious lie as to if he already knows it all. – Tevin C. R. Dubé

The paths unknown are initially so because not too many are willing to create new routes. But the unconventional paths are where trendsetters emerged unique and illustrious. – Tevin C. R. Dubé

We have created a lot of systems in Life in which we learn from but the system of Life that was created for us; many now have no time to learn about. –Tevin C. R. Dubé

Section Seven

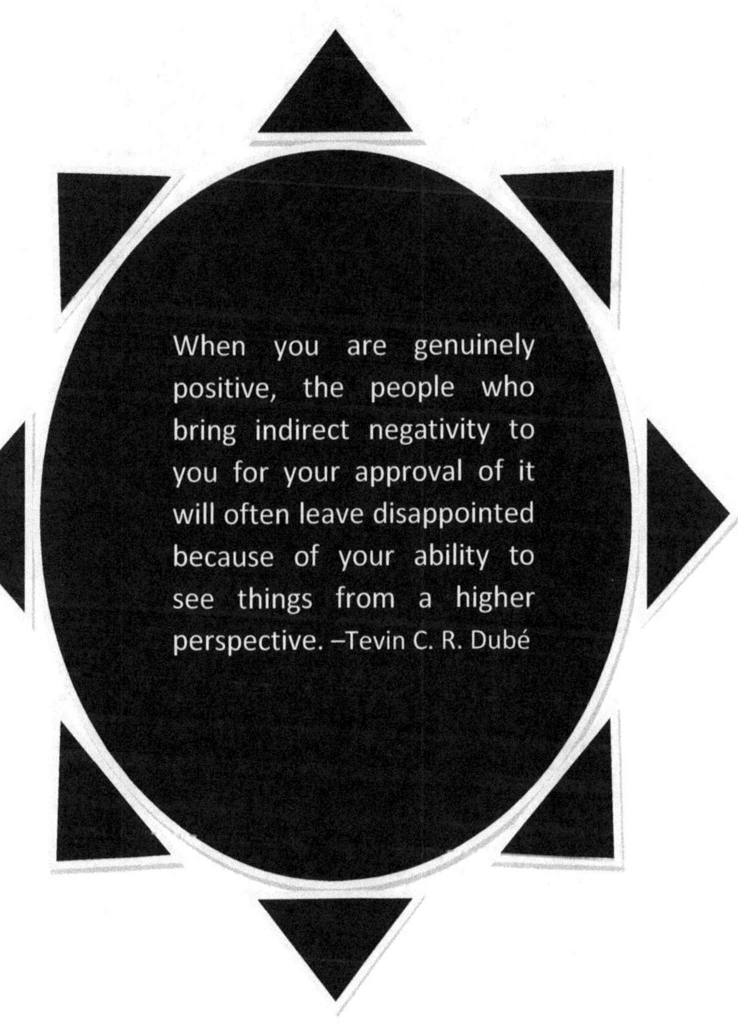
When you are genuinely positive, the people who bring indirect negativity to you for your approval of it will often leave disappointed because of your ability to see things from a higher perspective. –Tevin C. R. Dubé

Slavery did stole us away from our identity and history but spiritually; they could never truly tamper with the knowledge within that was responsible for the establishing of that which was in the beginning. –Tevin C. R. Dubé

The power that is within is far much greater than the power that is without. –Tevin C. R. Dubé

The people who are only in competition with others will never know the true divine bliss in being unique. When you become your own competition, there is no competition to be had. –Tevin C. R. Dubé

A tree that is detached from its roots will still remain fresh and green for an extended period of time. To disconnect yourself from Source will grant you the same but inevitably that too will wither away. –Tevin C. R. Dubé

Competition is fighting to be the best at doing the same thing. Being unique is being the best that you can be. That way, ordinary things will be done in unprecedented ways that weren't explored until you came along. –Tevin C. R. Dubé

The rewards of being unique are boundless and limitless. –Tevin C. R. Dubé

A lot of people don't grasp the true gravity about being unique. Being unique is being your authentic self. And since there will only ever be one of you, there is great universal merit in being yourself. –Tevin C. R. Dubé

When you are innately focused upon being the best version of yourself in every manner possible, if not giving sound advice, your time will become too expensive for constant frivolous tendencies. –Tevin C. R. Dubé

A tree without roots is surely lifeless so to be a human with a beating heart and still be heartless is to still be devoid of Life even though still breathing. –Tevin C. R. Dubé

When you don't learn to be you, you will always be lost among the crowd of lookalikes. But in being you, you can easily be distinguished because your trademark and characteristics would be indelible. –Tevin C. R. Dubé

Being your genuine self will always carry an energy that is original and unique in nature to you. The more you cultivate yourself is the greater your gifts will flourish and grow. –Tevin C. R. Dubé

Even though we all came from Source the Source Energy within each of our possession are not identical to another. –Tevin C. R. Dubé

You and I are both in possession of that Divine Spark which animates our being. But the way in which It ignites us individually are yet still unfathomable to conceive even though we already have billions and trillions of examples. –Tevin C. R. Dubé

Everything may seem to be similar in nature but no two things are the same. It is the same in the spiritual, no two things are every truly the same even there. As above, so below. As in Heaven, so in Earth. As within, so within. –Tevin C. R. Dubé

The elements will remain the same according to their nature. But no two fires will light the same, no two water droplets are identical, no two winds blow the same and nothing in Earth or space is in exact proportion. It's amazing! –Tevin C. R. Dubé

Your divine duty was always to be yourself. To be anti-you is to unnaturally go against your own divinity. You weren't designed to be anything other than yourself. When you master yourself you can incorporate everything else. –Tevin C. R. Dubé

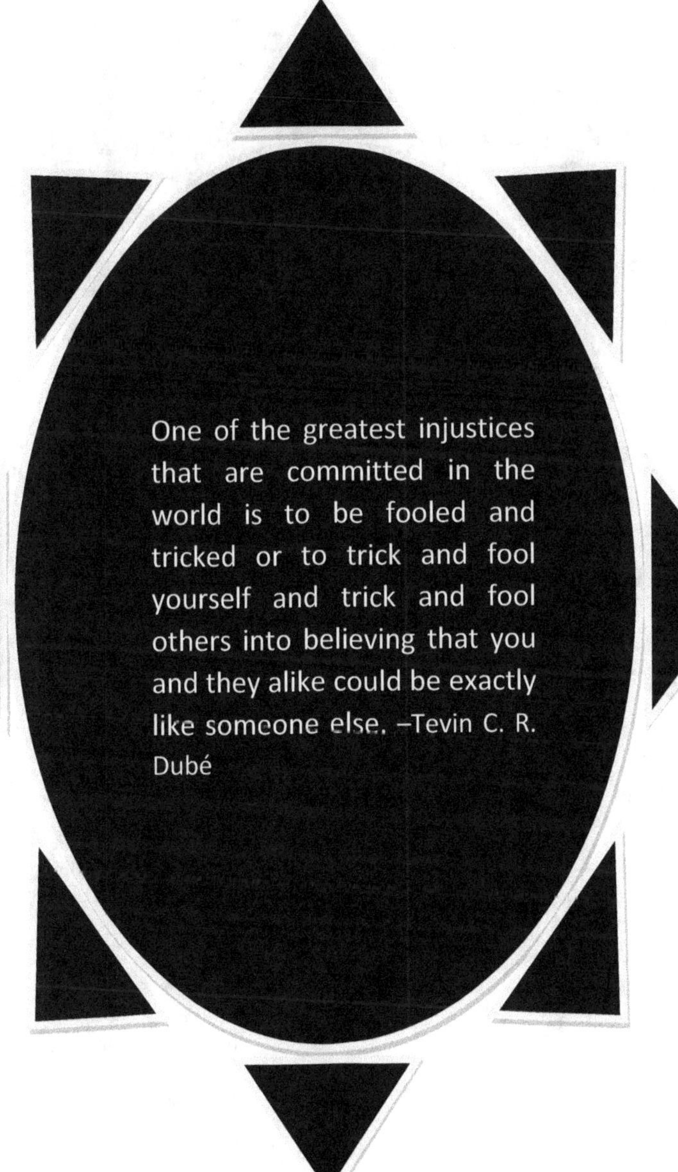
One of the greatest injustices that are committed in the world is to be fooled and tricked or to trick and fool yourself and trick and fool others into believing that you and they alike could be exactly like someone else. –Tevin C. R. Dubé

It is great to become inspired by others but it becomes self-sabotaging when you want to be exactly like them. You too are a limitless being so stop confining yourself to both limited thoughts and thinking. –Tevin C. R. Dubé

Death is an illusion. It is real but not real at the same time. –Tevin C. R. Dubé

You can learn to practice death while you're still alive not that you would need it when you actually die. You have to remember that you are the conscious awareness and not just the body. –Tevin C. R. Dubé

To practice death while you're still alive is to learn to still both the tongue and mind and just learn to be. The goal is to learn to just be aware and at peace and bliss within yourself. It is to meditate with stillness. –Tevin C. R. Dubé

Learning to consciously master death while you're alive is actually great practice to master being consciously alive after death. –Tevin C. R. Dubé

When you keep arriving at the overstanding that you are the conscious awareness behind your human identity, is the more you will keep identifying with your immortality and not just your carnal nature. –Tevin C. R. Dubé

Now that you have learned to identify yourself as a human being, try reintroducing your true spiritual self to your human self. All you have to do is learn to go within and trust the guidance of the Inner Voice of your intuition. –Tevin C. R. Dubé

To be scared of your spirituality is to be afraid of yourself. To be scared of your divinity is to be afraid to wield and harness your own power. –Tevin C. R. Dubé

To accept your humanity but reject your own spirituality is like a fish trying to swim without water. It's like a bird trying to soar without using its wings. It's like a dog that hates barking. –Tevin C. R. Dubé

Yes, your body belongs to you but if you don't learn to take control of your mind, you can become enslaved to just about anything that can easily overpower it. –Tevin C. R. Dubé

A consistently controlled state of mind is the source of ultimate power. –Tevin C. R. Dubé

When you learn to consistently control your mind, not only are you able to take control of frequencies but alter its vibration and energy. You can do as you please with any and all thoughts in general. –Tevin C. R. Dubé

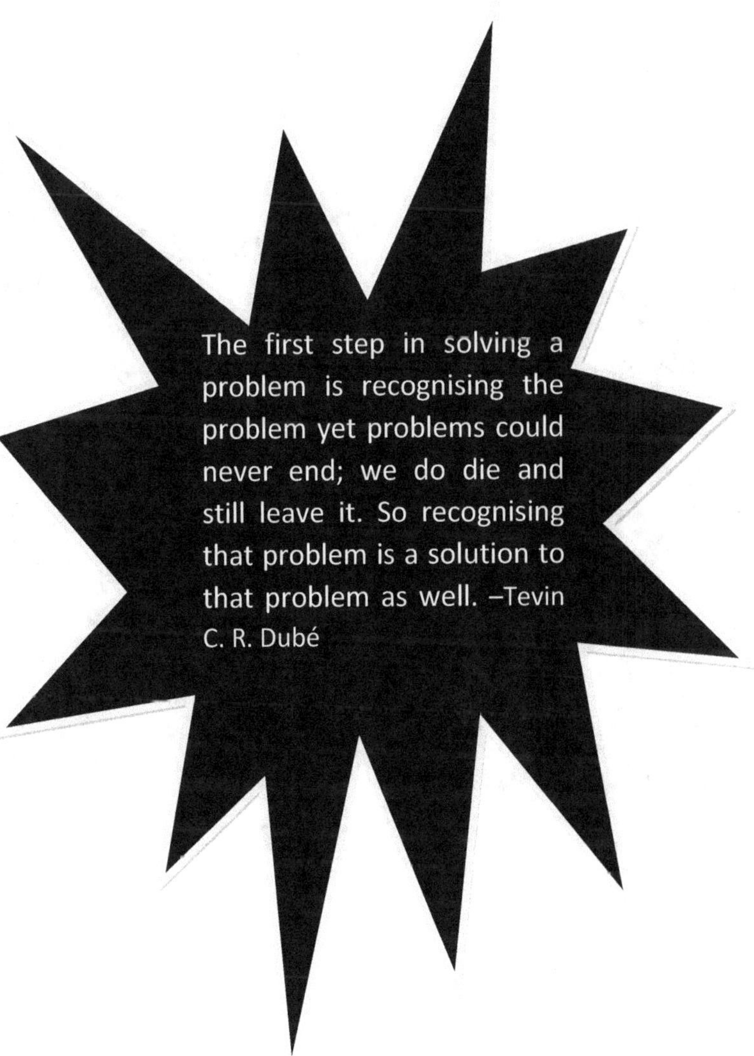
The first step in solving a problem is recognising the problem yet problems could never end; we do die and still leave it. So recognising that problem is a solution to that problem as well. –Tevin C. R. Dubé

To the Source we are all reporting back unto with our personal experiences and all things felt. The good thing is that if you remain open to receive, you would see that it is a two-way communication stream. –Tevin C. R. Dubé

The Absolute Divine is all knowing but through all things, IT is perpetually learning about all. –Tevin C. R. Dubé

Never allow your blessings to spoil you so much that it makes you become a curse. –Tevin C. R. Dubé

The more you learn to connect with Source within yourself; you will ultimately become the awareness of that aspect that has been awakened individually but the more we awaken along the way as a collective, we all shall awake unto the fullness of The Source Divine Itself. Think of it as the human body; even though the toes and fingers and cells operate individually, together it completes the entire structure and overall function of the body. At this stage, The Divine is somewhat in a handicapped state waiting for the rest of the parts to awake unto its full capacity. –Tevin C. R. Dubé

This entire existence called Life and Death is nothing but a one pointed dream or meditation by the Supreme Being of non-duality. We are the many characters that exist within the overall illusion but bits of the Divine Source is yet dormant within as the essence that animates our being and all of our reality. The more you turn internally and awaken unto who you truly are is the more The Divine leaves Its state of cosmic mediation. You are not your identity as much as you don't believe that you are in fact one and a part of The Divine itself. Therefore, if you can focus your thoughts as a one pointed mediation, you will awaken unto your attainment of Godhood. –Tevin C. R. Dubé

When you lucidly awake to yourself you become God in that you can consciously alter your dream state. And in your waking moments, the more you meditate and connect with the Divine Source within, you can alter reality by becoming the embodiment of God or Divinity within the flesh. –Tevin C. R. Dubé

Life is the most realistic dream ever. –Tevin C. R. Dubé

The kingdom of heaven is always at hand to whosoever meditates and learns to still the mind. –Tevin C. R. Dubé

When you fully overstand that your body is truly a temple, the cleaner you keep it, the stronger and purer the frequencies of the Absolute Divine, Angelic Beings, Ascended Masters and the Ancestors can be harboured and freely be displayed from within. –Tevin C. R. Dubé

Uncontrolled rage and anger is like a ravishing fire that consumes everything in its path. If you don't control these states of being, it will consume you in the process as well. It is a fire that consumes fire itself. – Tevin C. R. Dubé

If you don't learn to do for self, then you run the risk of imprisoning self. – Tevin C. R. Dubé

Love is the ultimate religion and gratitude is the ultimate prayer. – Tevin C. R. Dubé

Life is a challenge and preparation is essential. The problem is that most of us are already too prepared for the worse and don't challenge ourselves to be prepared for the best. – Tevin C. R. Dubé

Living your best dream or experiencing your worst nightmare is yet still internal. Experiencing bliss or torment is yet still mental. – Tevin C. R. Dubé

A snake is still a snake after shedding its skin. A dog will always be a dog no matter how good it is trained. Stop demanding the sun to come out at night. – Tevin C. R. Dubé

Every single breath should serve as a reminder that it is a wonderful gift to still be alive. – Tevin C. R. Dubé

What if we are the cells within a larger body and we are the transporters of energy within? What if all the ills happening within humanity are viruses due to cells (people) becoming infected? – Tevin C. R. Dubé

What if our Universe is just another cosmic being associating with other cosmic beings or Universes that makes up the multiverse in the same manner as our earthly human interaction? – Tevin C. R. Dubé

What if the multiplicity of Universes are but cells within a being that is beyond interacting with other beings that are beyond all our findings and discoveries? – Tevin C. R. Dubé

What if the Earth is sick because it is in its teenage state of rebellion and is suffering from a state of mental immaturity? What if it's being led astray by the negative influences of its planetary peers? – Tevin C. R. Dubé

What if the Father (sun) and Mother (moon) of the Earth is disciplining their child (Earth) who is in an emotionally imbalanced state energetically? What if the chaos, fear and confusion within are as a result of such? – Tevin C. R. Dubé

What if when people die within Earth is in the same manner and reason why cells die each day within the average human body? – Tevin C. R. Dubé

What if the same way the body of a human clinically dies but various activities still takes place within is the perfect scenario that equates to our current existence of Life and Decay? What if the Earth is clinically proven so? – Tevin C. R. Dubé

What if in the same manner you try to keep hope and faith alive by being consistently positive and productive are the same requirements required to keep the Earth and all of humanity alive? – Tevin C. R. Dubé